Supporting People with Intellectual Disabilities to Have a Good Life as They Grow Older

A self-study guide

Christine Towers

Supporting People with Intellectual Disabilities to Have a Good Life as They Grow Older
A self-study guide

© Pavilion Publishing and Media Ltd

The author has asserted her rights in accordance with the Copyright, Designs and Patents Act (1988) to be identified as the author of this work.

Published by:
Pavilion Publishing and Media Ltd
Blue Sky Offices
Cecil Pashley Way
Shoreham by Sea
West Sussex
BN43 5FF
Tel: 01273 434 943
Email: info@pavpub.com

Published 2019

A catalogue record for this book is available from the British Library.

ISBN: 978-1-912755-51-6

Pavilion is the leading training and development provider and publisher in the health, social care and allied fields, providing a range of innovative training solutions underpinned by sound research and professional values. We aim to put our customers first, through excellent customer service and value.

Author: Christine Towers
Production editor: Mike Benge, Pavilion Publishing and Media Ltd.
Cover design: Emma Dawe, Pavilion Publishing and Media Ltd.
Page layout: Emma Dawe, Pavilion Publishing and Media Ltd.
Photographs: Leyton Road Centre, Merton
Printing: CMP Digital Print Solutions

Contents

Introduction

Why training on good support for people with learning disabilities who are growing older is important

People with learning disabilities are living longer, and it is only within recent decades that many people with learning disabilities have begun to live into their 60s and beyond. Furthermore, until relatively recently, people with learning disabilities have aged while living with their families or in residential homes. It is now increasingly common for people with learning disabilities to be living more independent lives and are therefore ageing in supported living, either in shared houses or flats, or in their own flat, with a wide variety in levels of support.

The recent nature of this longer life expectancy and people aging in more independent settings means that there is limited knowledge about how best to adapt support for people as they age to ensure they can enjoy opportunities and feel safe and well in later life. Expectations have also increased for people's quality of life and, whether people are living in supported living, residential or nursing care, there is an understanding that people have the right to person-centred support that provides opportunities and promotes well-being.

This book and the training pack that can be used alongside it, aim to contribute to the development of our knowledge about supporting people as they age; to raise the expectations of older people with learning disabilities and their families and friends; and to raise the aspirations of individuals and services providing support.

Another reason why this training is important is discrimination and isolation. While these are often experienced by people in the general population as they age, they are particularly true for people who haven't been in a position to build up assets (such as a home of their own or a work-based pension) during their adult life. People with learning disabilities face discrimination and exclusion throughout their lives and potentially face the double jeopardy of being older with limited assets and having a learning disability.

There has been huge steps forward in recent years to end age discrimination, and generally there is an acceptance that society must give people the opportunity to age well. There is a plethora of information on ageing well and 'active ageing' covering aspects of life such as physical health, positive mental health, keeping active, being safe at home and maintaining independence for as long as possible. There is much to be learned from this approach to provide good support to people with learning disabilities as they age, and this book is shaped by the idea that people with learning disabilities have the same right to 'active ageing' or ageing well as anyone else.

Another potential reason for exclusion is the separate nature of support for older people in the general population and support for people with learning disabilities who are older. Older people with learning disabilities sometimes fall between the services offered for older people and those for people with learning disabilities, whereas in older age they may benefit from joined up thinking from across both support pathways. It is hoped the approach to providing good support in these training resources will build links across services for people with learning disabilities and older people more generally.

The purpose of this training resource

The purpose of this training is to contribute to improving the quality of life of people with learning disabilities as they grow older, through improving the quality of support they receive. This study guide offers good practice ideas in relation to accessing opportunities to have an active and enjoyable life while also being supported to be safe and well. The information should be useful for anyone providing support to people with learning disabilities as they get older, and also to those managing support services, commissioning support, and shaping and reviewing care and support plans. It will be a useful handbook for personal assistants, support workers and senior workers in supported living, residential and respite care and day opportunity services.

This study guide may also be helpful for family carers to think about what support they would like their relative to receive whether they live in the family home or elsewhere to know what good support should look like and to check the quality of the support their relative is receiving, and also to have conversations with their relative to decide the best use of support hours or to discuss at an annual review of a care and support plan or an assessment of need.

These training resources could also be used by community and voluntary organisations looking to be more inclusive of older people with learning disabilities, and by support services for older people who want to improve their offer to older people with learning disabilities.

It is also hoped that using these training resources will increase the job satisfaction experienced by support workers and others in services and organisations. There is significant scope to engage with people to find out how they are experiencing older age, looking together for solutions to difficulties and being led as much as possible by the person to achieve what they would like from older age. This should create an ongoing learning cycle for support workers thereby increasing their knowledge and skills as well as enjoyment at work. This approach doesn't necessarily require more resources, only for them to be used differently, and good outcomes can be achieved even when people are only receiving a low level of support.

The underlying values of the training resources

People have the right to a good life made up of being safe and well alongside having opportunities to do enjoyable and meaningful activities. Support should be based on a basic right to have choice and control, maintain as much independence as wanted, and be able to participate in groups and activities that are of interest to the person and to learn new things.

This training is underpinned by three key approaches:

- Person-centred thinking and planning to help understand what really matters to a person, building on their strengths, ensuring they are listened to and are at the centre of decision-making about what happens in their life.

- Good communication with the person being supported, and others who know them well.

- Encouraging participation, choice-making and independence.

Most of the exercises promote a practical approach to improving the quality of support and encourage participants to note how their learning can improve their day-to-day practice. All of the ideas in the exercises can be adapted for people with more severe or profound levels of disability, but they are likely to require supporters to use specific approaches in communication that they know work for the person, as well as talking to others who know them well.

How they were developed

The materials are based on current knowledge about what supports people with learning disabilities to have a good life as they age. Some of this evidence comes from research papers, while other evidence comes from talking with people with learning disabilities about their experience of ageing and what was important to them in the support they received. Further corroboration came from the author's experience of delivering a quality assurance programme across a wide range of support services as well as developing and managing services over many years.

As these training resources were being developed, the author talked with people with learning disabilities about what is important to them as they get older. At two centres that provided day time opportunities for older people with learning disabilities, she explored ideas such as what helped them to remain active, how they liked to be supported to look after their health and ways in which they would like to remember family and friends who had died. In addition, Ian Davies, who has been an active self-advocate for around 30 years, shared his experiences of growing older and his thoughts on good support. He also contributed to the filming for the video clips used in the training materials.

What was apparent from talking to Ian and the other people who contributed, is that people with learning disabilities have very little opportunity to speak on their own or as a group about growing older and the support they would like to have to continue to enjoy life and to feel safe and well. Before working on these training materials, Ian hadn't spoken in any depth about growing older and, after doing so, he was clear about the importance of people being given the opportunities to talk and be listened to. The training therefore has a focus on encouraging conversations about growing older. Some people will be able to engage in verbal conversations, perhaps with the help of images, photographs and objects. For others it will mean spending time with a person to get a sense of what's important to them, what works and doesn't work in relation to organising support, and talking with people who know them well.

The structure of the training materials

There are two parts to the training materials: this self-study guide and a separate training manual. The manual is a guide for leading group-based training. Both parts of the training materials cover the same topics and have similar material and exercises.

Self-study guide

This self-study guide is designed for people to use on their own, either for their independent learning or as part of training and development within a service or organisation. Whichever route you are following, it is important to have someone with whom you can discuss your reflections, ideas and learning. If you are studying as part of your work you should aim to discuss your learning in supervision time, team meetings if appropriate, and hopefully there will also be time for group feedback and discussions with fellow learners. If you are studying independently you could find a mentor, colleague or 'study buddy' with whom to discuss your learning.

The training covers six topics:

- Understanding growing older.
- Emotional well-being.
- Health.
- Being active and involved.
- Home life.
- Bereavement and dying.

The first chapter is an introduction to the key ideas around growing older and what this may mean in the lives of people with learning disabilities. The other five chapters cover key aspects of people's lives as they grow older.

Each chapter stands on its own although it would be recommended to study them in the order they are presented. Completing the six chapters will take around seven hours of learning although it would be preferable to break this up into either three or six sessions. Allocating time to think about the reflections and tasks will maximise learning opportunities and the development of ideas that can be transferred to your place of work.

Each chapter starts with the aim and learning outcomes. This is followed by an introduction and three exercises to explore different aspects of the topic. Each exercise has a short task which provides an opportunity to use your learning to build a portfolio of ideas for you to use in your support setting. Some of the chapters have video clips to play. Some of these are of Ian Davies talking about his experience of growing older and others are of the author sharing her learning from talking with people with learning disabilities and supporting people who are growing older.

At the end of the guide there are links to resources and recommended further reading for people who would like to continue to learn more (page 73). Some of these are referred to at relevant points in the topics.

The training pack

The training pack is designed for group-based learning and includes:

- PowerPoint presentations for the training.
- Suggestions for how to deliver the training, including exercises, learning cycle questions to look at a topic in more depth, and tips for trainers to help them deliver the training.
- There are links to the videos of the author and Ian Davies to reinforce the learning in topics.
- Learning resources with additional information and templates to write down ideas from exercises.
- A participant's learning portfolio.
- A copy of the self-study guide.

The film clips

Throughout this book you will be directed to watch certain film clips to enhance the specific learning point being discussed, and there also suggestions for other clips that can be watched optionally. All the clips are available at www.pavpub.com/supporting-older-people-resources.

In these film clips you will meet Christine Towers, the author of the training materials, and Ian Davies, a self advocate.

Now might be a good time to watch **Film Clip 1.1: Introducing Christine and Ian.**

Chapter 1: Understanding growing older

Aim and learning outcomes

The aim of this chapter is to gain an understanding of the different aspects of growing older and how people with learning disabilities may experience them.

It will help you to:

- Gain a broad understanding of what is meant by 'growing older'.

- Understand how people with learning disabilities usually approach older age with disadvantages when compared with the rest of the population.

- Gain good practice ideas when supporting people with learning disabilities as they get older.

Introduction: understanding growing older

This book and the training that accompanies it focuses on the changes people experience as they get older and provides ideas for helping people to have a good quality of life, helping them have a positive experience of ageing and enabling them to remain as active and involved as possible. The book specifically addresses the period of life before people become more frail and may need a much higher level of care to prevent them from being at risk. However, much of the content could also be relevant at this time of life.

This opening chapter looks at what growing older means in the lives of people with learning disabilities, and it explores key approaches for providing people with support that is enjoyable and meaningful.

There are three exercises on the topic of understanding growing older for you to read and then undertake short tasks:

1. What does growing older mean to you?

2. The experience of ageing for people with learning disabilities.

3. Key approaches to providing good support to age well.

1. What does growing older mean to you?

Growing older is something we all experience and our thoughts about this will depend on many different factors such as our own age, the age of people we are connected to as well as our background and culture.

Reflection

What does 'growing older' mean to you? Think about your family and friends: whom amongst them do you think of as getting older, and why?

There are two ways of looking at ageing. It can be seen as:

1. Adding on years, which is the chronological process of ageing.

2. A loss of function or ability over time, which is the biological process of ageing.

The loss of function and ability is only loosely related to chronological age. Therefore, reaching a certain age does not correspond with needing help with certain tasks or finding specific activities more difficult.

There is no specific age at which people are described as 'older', but the ages of 60 and 65 are often used to define 'seniors', and this term is loosely related to previous retirement ages. However, in 2012 the default age of retirement of 65 was abolished and the age of entitlement to state pension has been increasing in stages in the light of longer life expectancy.

A key point is that people with learning disabilities usually experience biological processes of ageing at a younger chronological age than the rest of the population.

Watch **Film Clip 1.2: People age differently,** which explains that getting older cannot be defined as reaching a specific age but is a process with numerous gradual or sudden changes over time.

It is important to remember that change may not just be in one direction, for example people may regain skills after a period of illness or after living with pain. It is also important to recognise that there will be many variations between people who are of a similar age. Therefore, what is important to think about, for example, for one 60-year-old person you support may not be relevant to another person of a similar age.

2. The experience of ageing for people with learning disabilities

In this exercise you will gain an understanding of both the similarities and possible differences that people with learning disabilities may experience as they grow older compared with the general population.

Many of the experiences of people with learning disabilities as they age will be similar to those of the general population. However, there are also significant differences they are likely to experience.

Similarities

George	Reg
■ Is now 66 and finds he has started slowing down. ■ He spends more time at home and enjoys watching football on the TV and gardening. ■ He meets his friends for a drink in the pub. ■ He has aches and pains in his knees and is worried about his hearing getting worse.	■ Is now 66 and finds he has a lot less energy than a few years ago. ■ He sees his friends at the day centre twice a week. ■ He spends more time at home now and enjoys watching sport and day-time TV. ■ He is worried about his diet as he has been told he eats too many sugary foods and his blood sugar level is high.

What do you think when you read the similarities between George and Reg's lives?

Now read the differences between their lives.

Differences

George	Reg
■ He retired last year after working for the Royal Mail for 40 years and receives a good pension. ■ His wife recently died but he has two grown up children, one of whom has children and lives within driving distance. His friends regularly call to take him out for a drink to help him cope with his loss.	■ Until recently he volunteered one day a week at the hospital but it became too much and he no longer goes. He went to the day centre on three other days but now only goes twice a week. ■ He moved to a Housing Association flat after his mother's death and is now worried what is going to happen as he is finding the external stairs difficult to walk up.

continued →

George	Reg
■ He and his wife bought a small house where he still lives, but he may move next year to be nearer to his daughter. ■ He sees a private physiotherapist once every two weeks to exercise his knee and he has made an appointment to get his hearing tested.	■ His close friend at the day centre recently died and, although no-one knows, this has made him feel even more lonely. ■ A support worker comes to the house twice a week and helps him sort out bills, shopping and cleaning. ■ He missed his last appointment at the diabetes clinic as he didn't understand the appointment letter.

Task: Similarities and differences

First, write down what strikes you about the similarities and differences of George's and Reg's lives?

Next, think about why might Reg's life experiences make older age more difficult for him than for George? Write down two or three ideas.

Now look at the suggestions below.

	Disadvantages for Reg
Financial	He hasn't had paid work so has probably had a much lower level of disposable income during his adult life, nor will he have accumulated savings. He doesn't have a work-based pension and will continue to be dependent on state benefits.
Friends and relationships	Reg is less likely to have a friendship group with access to a range of assets, and less likely to have had a long-term relationship or had children and grandchildren.
Support network	His support network comes from less mixed support and is more likely to come from paid supporters and possibly extended family rather than a partner, grown-up children, friends or colleagues.
Emotional support	Reg doesn't have anyone to turn to for emotional support. He is grieving for his friend but no-one at the centre has picked up on this so he doesn't have anyone to talk to about it.
Housing	He doesn't own the flat where he lives so doesn't know what will happen to his home when he can no longer manage the stairs to reach his flat. He doesn't know how his support would be arranged if he lived somewhere else or whether he would need to share a flat with others.
Health	He experiences a lack of reasonable adjustments to ensure access to health care, and he has less money to do activities that are beneficial to his health and well-being.

3. Three key approaches to good support for ageing well

There are three key approaches that underpin the content in this study guide, which can all contribute to people having better opportunities as they age and will help to compensate for the lack of opportunities that may have been experienced, as discussed above.

Figure 1.1: Three approaches

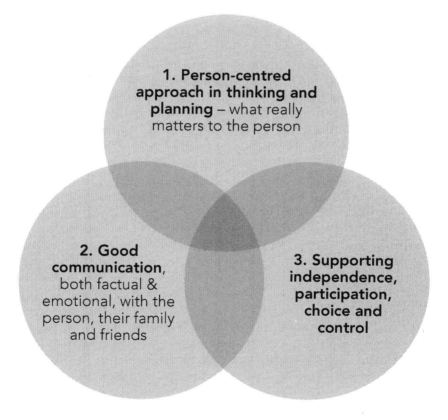

Person-centred thinking and planning

Person-centred thinking and planning help you to understand what really matters to a person, and to ensure that they are listened to and are at the centre of decision-making about what happens in their life. You may have learnt about using person-centred planning approaches in previous training, in which case you should have some useful planning tools that can be adapted to have conversations with people and record information. Throughout this book there are references to a variety of person-centred approaches and links to useful tools such as using a relationship map, supporting people to participate in their community and finding out what is important to a person. Person-centred information needs to be gathered and regularly updated to inform each person's individual support plan and to inform decision-making.

Good communication

Getting support right is all about good communication with the person you are supporting, and with others who know them well. Good communication should cover both factual and emotional communication. The latter is often overlooked but is particularly important at a time when people are usually facing many significant changes. You need to be aware that, as people age, the way in which they receive and give information often changes. You are therefore likely to need to adapt the way in which you communicate in order to respond to people's changing needs. Being a good communicator is about finding ways to share information and ideas as well as actively listening to a person, whether through words or body language. Most people will find it helpful and reassuring to have conversations about growing older and any changes that are occurring. Each chapter in this book has information and exercises that should help you have these conversations.

Supporting independence, participation, choice and control

Watch **Film Clip 1.4: Encouraging independence**. At the heart of good support is encouraging a person's participation, choice-making and independence. It is often easier to step in and do things or make decisions for a person. However, over time this leads the person to become more dependent on paid support and lowers their self-confidence and self-esteem. As people age there may seem an increasing need to step in, yet supporting a person to be active and engaged in meaningful activities and making choices will maintain their confidence and sense of well-being. For older people with learning disabilities, 'active ageing' may mean getting the support they need to have choice and control in their life and to have valued roles at home and in their community but using the ideas in this book will help you to find out what it means for each person you support.

These three approaches are interrelated and will all contribute to developing good practice and help people to overcome some of the disadvantages they are likely to have experienced, as discussed in the previous exercise. The information and exercises in the following five chapters aim to build your skills and knowledge in these key areas.

Reflection

Look back at Reg's situation and think how these key approaches might help Reg.

Your learning from this chapter

To finish, complete the summary below.

These are the main points that I have learnt from this chapter and would like to use to develop my practice:

Chapter 2: Emotional well-being

Aim and learning outcomes

The aim of this chapter is to give you an understanding about the emotional well-being of people you support in relation to growing older.

It will help you to:

- gain confidence in finding out how people feel as they get older

- understand the importance of people's histories and memories

- become familiar with tools to help people feel positive about the future.

Introduction: what is emotional well-being as you grow older?

Everyone is different in how they respond emotionally to growing older and the changes this is likely to involve. Some people may feel there are things in their life that have got better while others may feel their life is getting more difficult and may be worried about this. They could also be experiencing a mixture of these emotions.

Some changes may be difficult but may also open up new opportunities, for example the death of a parent may lead to deep feelings of loss, but may also lead to someone gaining confidence and independence from living in their own flat or with friends for the first time.

This is what some of the people who contributed to this training said would help them to feel good about their life as they get older:

'I want to have people I can talk to.'

'I want to feel safe. I want to be well-supported.'

'I want to enjoy myself and learn new things.'

'I don't want lots of worries.'

Your role can be to help people share how they are feeling about growing older, covering both the:

- positive experiences and feelings of ageing

- aspects they are finding difficult or that they need reassurance about.

You can use this information to look at how support can be adapted to a person's changing feelings and needs.

Find out:	Support can:
What makes someone feel good about their life.	Build on a good thing e.g. make sure it continues, do more if it.
What does someone find worrying or difficult in their life.	Find solutions e.g. give information, explain why it's happening, reduce or remove difficulty.

In this chapter, there are three exercises to explore aspects of emotional well-being, including information for you to read and a number of short tasks to complete:

1. Finding out what growing older means for a person: positives, difficulties and worries.

2. Supporting people to record their history and memories.

3. Finding out about people's hopes and wishes.

1. Finding out what growing older means for a person: positives, difficulties and worries

There are different ways of finding out about what a person feels good about in their life and what are the difficulties and worries they have. The approach you choose will depend on factors such as a person's understanding and their preferred way of communicating.

Some people will have an understanding of what growing older means and will be able to explore their feelings about this while others will need your help to understand about the passing of time and how life can change. You may need to use resources such as photos, objects, story boards and photo stories. People with more complex support needs will need others to be involved in gathering person-centred information.

It is usually beneficial to start by exploring the good things people are experiencing as they get older or what they enjoy about their life at the moment. This helps to make it a more enjoyable conversation for the person and to make it seem different from meetings, such as assessments and reviews, that often focus on what is wrong and what is needed. The person you are supporting is likely to introduce the difficulties in their own time. Allow the person to lead the conversation and be an active listener.

Reflection

What is an active listener?

Being an active listener means paying attention to what a person is saying and not jumping in with your views. Reflect on what someone is saying to you by using phrases such as: 'It sounds like you are saying...' or, 'Tell me a bit more about why that is important to you...'

Think about how you could be better at listening when you are talking with someone you support. Write down two ways to be a better listener that you will try when at work.

Here are three approaches you could use to find out how someone feels about growing older:

- One-to-one conversations.
- Supporting a small group to explore together.
- A circle of support or a group of people coming together to use some person-centred planning tools and share ideas.

One-to-one conversations

Watch the **Film Clip 2.1: Opportunities to talk** talking about why it can be helpful to have conversations about growing older.

Fred's story

Fred is a man in his mid-60s who lives on his own. Talking to him about how he feels about getting older, he said he felt isolated and stuck in his ways. He said, 'I don't know what kind of future I've got'. During the conversation he mentioned that he has lots of worn-out shoes at home and when asked about these he said he used to do a lot of walking. He said he had stopped as he'd got older and more anxious.

This led to asking him if this was something he'd like to start doing again, perhaps with other people. For the first time in the conversation he smiled and looked interested and had questions about how this might be possible. Ideas such as looking for a rambling group or healthy walk programme in the area where he lives were discussed. His support worker searched on the local council's website and found free healthy walks taking place in nearby parks, which also encouraged participants to make new friends. Fred's support worker went along with him for the first few weeks and helped him to get to know the person who led the walks and others who regularly went along. Another man, in his 70s, who was feeling lonely since his wife had died, was also a regular on the walks. They both enjoyed each other's company and on weeks when there wasn't an organised walk they arranged to meet up for a walk of their own.

Supporting a small group to explore together

Some people may prefer to explore growing older with others such as a partner, friends, co-tenants or co-residents. This works best with a small group of around two to four people, otherwise people may lose the discussion thread or get bored. Talking as a small group provides an opportunity for people to listen to each other, which in turn can help people to understand and support each other.

In *Talking Together: Facilitating peer support activities to help people with learning disabilities understand about growing older and living with dementia* there is an outline for a group activity called 'Good things about growing older', which may provide you with some useful ideas to talk about this with a small group of people (details at the end of the chapter).

Circle of support or person-centred planning group

A group of people could meet together to share their knowledge of a person alongside using person-centred planning tools to gather information and ideas for the future. This could be helpful when a person would find it difficult to take part in a conversation perhaps because of profound disabilities or feelings of anxiety.

There are two templates in *I'm Thinking Ahead* (details at end of the chapter) called 'This is what I need to have a good life' and 'This is what I need to keep safe and well', which could be used to talk about and record person-centred information and would be particularly useful for a circle of support or person-centred planning group to use. They could be used to understand a person's changing needs as they get older.

Task: How will you find out?

Think about someone you support (or a couple, a group of friends, co-tenants, co-residents) and how you could find out how they are feeling about older age – the good things, the hard things and their worries.

Write down how you would approach this, what resources you might use and what would be the first steps you would take. Note enough detail so you could take this into work and discuss it with a supervisor or colleagues, or to follow up with the person.

2. Supporting people to record their history and memories

As we get older our experiences and memories from the past often become more important. Usually, they are something we enjoy talking about and give us a sense of the life we have lived.

Reflection

Why are your memories and your history important to you?

Do you do anything to record your memories or history?

There are many reasons why having a record of their history and memories may be important to someone with learning disabilities as they get older:

- It may help someone to remember their past; happy and sad events, people in their life and people they've lost.

- It may help someone to have a sense of who they are in the present.

- It tells others who they are, what's important to them now and in the past.

- It is a resource that aids conversations and connections with others.

- The information can help new people who they meet to see them as someone with a history, experiences and knowledge gained from life (i.e. more than an older person with learning disabilities).

However, sometimes people end up with few or no photos or objects to remember the past by, and this is more likely to be true of older people with learning disabilities who have previously lived in long-stay institutions or whose families have died. Sometimes support staff add to this problem by tidying and clearing people's rooms without attributing enough value to their belongings.

If you support people who are living with elderly family members or have moved from their family home but whose family are still alive, talk together about how they could support the gathering of memories. They may help their relative to choose objects such as ornaments or a piece of furniture they would like to be given now or to inherit later. They may be able to help with labelling photographs, recalling events or recording messages to accompany photographs.

There are lots of ways in which a person can be supported to record their history and memories, and below there are ideas about life story books, talking photo albums and memory boxes. It's important to adapt ideas so they work well for the person you are supporting and also to remember that all of these are owned by the person and not by a support service.

Life story books and memory boxes can start small and grow as and when a person is interested. They may gain more significance over time and in response to other life changes such as moving home or developing dementia.

Developing a life story book, talking photo album or memory box also helps people to understand the passage of time, giving people a sense of their past compared with the present. This can help when talking with people about how they feel as they grow older (as in the first exercise in this chapter). You could use them as a way to help people understand about the passing of time and how their life is changing as they get older.

Life story books

Life story books are a way of recording important or significant people, places or events that have happened in someone's life.

Play **Film Clip 2.2: Marcus' life story**.

Reflection

How do you think Marcus' life book could be used to help him have a better life? Write down two or three of your ideas.

Here are some things to think about when supporting someone to develop a life story book:

- It does not need to start at the beginning but can be built around a few memories a person tells you about (or that others tell you). Over time this may build into a 'book'. A digital or a lose-leaf format is therefore best so it can be added to.

- Photos can be scanned and added, preferably with captions to help with reminiscing and conversations.

- The book can just be for the person themselves to look at, or something they may want to share with others (and this may vary at different times). It's important to talk with the person about this to help them decide whether or not to include certain information.

Talking photo albums

These are photo albums where messages or information can be recorded to go with photos. The voice on the recording could be that of someone they feel close to, which would add to their memories.

These can be bought on the internet through various organisations (search for talking photo albums) or through www.talkingproducts.com/

Memory boxes

Memory boxes are a way of putting together objects that have meaning to a person and that they can look at on their own or with support. The development of a memory box can be an enjoyable and creative activity.

Here are a few things to think about when supporting someone to develop a memory box:

- The choice of container can reflect how the person would like the memory box to work for them, for example it could be an attractive box or small case or a set of drawers for stationary that would provide separate compartments. An empty shoebox could be used and decorated to reflect the person's interests or personality. The container can be part of the memory.

- It is a good idea to include written information about the meaning of the objects to serve as a reminder, or to be shared with others. It could also include instructions on how to use the memory box with the person.

- One of the advantages of memory boxes is that they can be multi-sensory and if someone has, for example, a visual impairment, the objects can relate to their senses of touch and smell, for example pebbles from a beach or the perfume of a favourite person. If someone has profound and multiple disabilities think about which senses are particularly important to them and how they might best experience and remember people and events, for example recordings of voices or music.

- Memory boxes are often enjoyed by people after developing dementia because of their sensory nature and as a reminder of significant past memories.

Task: making a memory box for yourself

Think about what you would put in a memory box. You could draw an outline of your 'container' and then either draw or write what you would put in it. Or you could find a box or other container and gather things to put inside. If you are planning to ask people you support whether they would like a memory box then it is a good idea to make one to take along to help people understand the idea.

After you have done this task, answer the following reflection questions.

> **Reflection**
>
> How did you feel about drawing or making the memory box? Did it help you to think about significant people, places and events?
>
> For people who do not have families to help them collect their memories or do not have photos, it can be painful to think and talk about the past. How might you approach this? Do you think it is preferable to find ways to look at this or rather to avoid painful pasts?

In *Talking Together: Facilitating peer support activities to help people with learning disabilities understand about growing older and living with dementia* there is an activity on p19 for making memory boxes (see resources at end of chapter).

3. Finding out about people's hopes and wishes

Supporting people to think about their hopes and wishes can help them look beyond their day-to-day activities, feel positive about the future, be active and engaged and try new things as they get older.

As people in general get older, they often begin to think about what they'd like to do in their remaining years, and retirement is often a trigger for this. Most people with learning disabilities do not have this transition into retirement that might prompt a conversation with family, friends or support workers, and so are likely to need support to realise they could have opportunities to try new things. Support workers can therefore play a valuable role in exploring a person's wish list. This list might include:

- things they haven't had a chance to do but would like to before it's too late

- learning something new

- reconnecting with people and places from the past.

Hopes and wishes can be something quite small, or something more aspirational. Someone may like to explore a new shop, shopping centre, park or garden where they don't usually go. There may be someone they'd like to visit who they haven't seen for a while or a place they'd like to go to that they remember from past holidays.

People's hopes and wishes may not seem realistic or easily achievable to you, but the idea can be planned for in stages or explored to find something related that is achievable. Encourage people to have aspirations in their older age and then think creatively to find ways to make them happen.

Some people will not be able to respond to questions about their hopes and wishes so you could then approach this by getting together a group of people who know them well, such as a circle of support, and thinking together about what their wishes might be, trying things out and learning from the experience.

Talking about hopes and wishes is not a one-off conversation but something to return to. When people are first asked about their hopes and wishes, they often do not immediately come up with an answer, but it is still an important question to ask. Even if somebody is happy with the way their life is and doesn't make suggestions, it is likely that being asked this question helps them to know that people who support them care that they are enjoying life and they have a right to opportunities in older age. They may also feel encouraged to speak up when they have an idea or when you ask them again.

Helpful resource

I'm Thinking Ahead has a template 'My hopes and wishes' (see resources at end of the chapter).

Task: hopes and wishes

Think about someone you support who is older and consider how you might find out about their hopes and wishes. This could be the person you wrote about in the first exercise or someone different.

Use *Learning Resource 1: Hopes and wishes* on page 70 to write down your ideas in relation to these questions:

■ What communication tools will you use?

■ What would be a good setting?

■ Who else might you involve (family, friends, others who know the person well)?

■ How will you record what you find out and make a plan for achieving their hopes and wishes (e.g. pictures, voices, photographs)?

One more thought

Supporting people's emotional well-being needs on-going conversations. Over time people may become more confident about thinking of ideas to help them with ageing.

Keep a note of what people say so their thoughts don't get lost, and so that ideas can be followed up and further conversations can take place.

Your learning from this chapter

To finish this chapter, complete the summary below.

These are the main points that I have learnt from this chapter and would like to use to develop my practice:

Resources

Talking Together: Facilitating peer support activities to help people with learning disabilities understand about growing older and living with dementia (2015). There are two activities which may be particularly useful: 'Activity 7: Good things about growing older' and 'Activity 19: Memory boxes'. This resource is available to download for free at: www.togethermatters.org.uk

I'm Thinking Ahead (2016) includes a section on 'How to plan', with templates for 'This is what I need to have a good life', 'This is what I need to keep safe and well' and 'My hopes and wishes for the future'. These can be used to think about what someone needs and wants as they grow older. This resource is available to download for free at: www.togethermatters.org.uk

Chapter 3: Health

Aim and learning outcomes

The aim of this chapter is to give you an understanding of how to support people to live healthy lives and receive the health care they need as they get older.

It will help you to:

- Be familiar with the common health problems people may experience as they age.

- Understand the importance of preventing ill-health and reducing the risk of serious illness.

- Support people to receive the health treatment they need in older age.

Introduction: good support with health

Having good health is about much more than being well: it touches every area of life helping people to feel positive, go out and about, be active, meet people and take part in a wide range of activities at home and elsewhere. On the other hand, poor health can lead to many limitations, restrict activity and impair the enjoyment of many aspects of life.

People with learning disabilities have an increased likelihood of experiencing health problems, and having them to a greater degree than the general population. This is because of factors such as poorer healthcare, lack of accessible information about healthy lifestyles, and lack of finances and support to make healthy choices and have a good diet.

A startling fact is that people with learning disabilities die, on average, at a considerably younger age than the general population. A recent report by LeDeR highlighted this with data that showed females with learning disabilities die 27 years younger than the rest of the population and males 23 years younger (for more information, see Resources and references on page 37). There have been many reports in recent years to improve the healthcare received by people with learning disabilities, but this significant gap still remains.

There are many different actions that can be taken to help people with learning disabilities live healthier lives. Figure 3.1 below shows a person with learning disabilities at the centre of three key elements that can be delivered by support workers and support organisations to contribute to people living healthier lives as they get older:

■ Being aware of common health problems people may experience as they get older.

■ Preventing ill-health and reducing risks of serious health problems.

■ Ensuring people get the right health care in later life.

Figure 3.1:

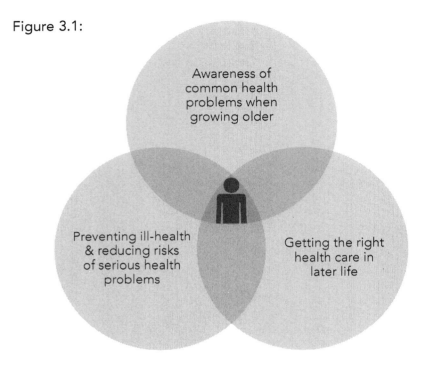

In this chapter there are three exercises that relate to the diagram above, with information for you to read and a number of short tasks to complete:

1. Health problems to be aware of as people age.

2. Preventing ill-health and reducing risks of serious health problems.

3. Supporting people to get the right healthcare in later life.

1. Health problems to be aware of as people age

It is important for support staff to be aware of possible health problems as a person ages, as people with learning disabilities may not be able to describe or indicate changes they are experiencing or pain they are feeling.

Task: Common health problems

Make a list of the common health problems that people you support have experienced as they got older, or that you think they may experience in the future.

Now look at *Table 3.1: Common health changes, conditions and diseases to be aware of* on page 30. This lists a range of health problems that increase with age as well as the illnesses that people with learning disabilities have a greater risk of. An example of this is that women with Down's syndrome may have an early menopause, leading to a greater risk of osteoporosis. People with Down's syndrome are also at greater risk of early onset of Alzheimer's disease. In addition, people with learning disabilities more generally get dementia at a younger average age than the general population.

Write down your ideas about how you might use this list of common health problems in your work or in your organisation.

What are your thoughts when you see this list? Are the health problems ones you have come across before in your work?

Of course, not everyone will experience these health problems but some people will be experiencing more than one of them at any one time.

Table 3.1: Common health changes, conditions and diseases to be aware of

	Changes to look for
Sensory	Common eye problems include cataracts, glaucoma and macular degeneration. Changes to vision including difficulty seeing in low light. Difficulty hearing higher pitched voices and sounds and hearing in busy places. Accumulation of earwax. Changes in taste and smell.
Digestive system	Digestion of food more difficult. Swallowing and digestive reflexes slow down. Swallowing may become more difficult. Problems with reflux. Constipation.
Kidneys and urinary tract	Kidneys become less efficient. Diabetes and high blood pressure can cause damage to kidneys. Greater risk of kidney failure among people with learning disabilities. Urinary incontinence can be a symptom of hormone levels in women and enlarged prostate in men.
Weight	Lower levels of physical activity and a slowing metabolism may contribute to weight gain. Some drugs, including anti-psychotic drugs, can lead to weight gain. Weight loss may occur as result of swallowing difficulties or a loss of appetite. May be an indication of an underlying illness such as cancer. Greater risk of obesity among people with learning disabilities.
Posture and movement	Bones shrink in size and density and are more prone to fractures and osteoporosis. Muscles, tendons and joints may lose strength and flexibility. Poorer balance leading to an increased risk of falls.
Hair, skin and nails	Skin becomes drier and more brittle. Lower level of sweating results in greater susceptibility to heat stroke and heat exhaustion. Hair and nails grow slower and become brittle needing a higher level of attention.
Heart, lungs and circulatory system	High blood pressure (hypertension) – swollen ankles can be a symptom. Atherosclerosis (hardening of arteries). Greater risk of heart disease, hypertension, stroke and respiratory diseases (such as pneumonia). Aspiration pneumonia as a result of matter from the stomach or mouth getting into the lungs.
Brain and nervous system	Brain cells decrease leading to memory loss. Can also lead to reflexes slowing down, co-ordination difficulties and being more easily distracted. There is a greater risk of dementia among people with learning disabilities.

continued ➜

	Changes to look for
Mental health and well-being	Changes in sleep patterns. Sleep problems can be an indication of poor health or chronic health problems. Increase in anxiety and depression.
Sepsis	Although sepsis is rare it is important to have an awareness of it as the signs are often missed yet the infection needs to be treated urgently. It can quickly lead to severe sepsis or septic shock which, in turn, can cause organ failure and death. The person may not have a fever or high temperature but just feel very unwell. People with learning disabilities may have a number of pre- conditions that put them at greater risk.
Thyroid disease	The incidence of thyroid problems increases with age but is sometimes difficult to diagnose as there may be a reduced number of symptoms or they may not be as obvious as those in younger patients. Hypothyroidism (under-active thyroid) is the most common thyroid condition in people over 60 years of age: symptoms, such as confusion, memory loss, depression, falling, heart failure and constipation are frequently missed as they are also signs of common illnesses of older people.

Reflection

How do you think people who experience many of these symptoms may be feeling? Do you think they may feel overwhelmed, depressed or in need of reassurance? How might you help someone to cope with these feelings?

2. Preventing ill-health and reducing risks of serious health problems

Support workers can make a significant difference to the prevention of ill health and the reduction in risk of serious health problems in later life. There are two aspects to prevention:

■ Preventing the onset of illness or injury.

■ Early diagnosis and prompt treatment to prevent more serious illness.

Reflection

What do you think helps to prevent ill-health or reduces the risks of serious ill health? Think about the steps you take in your own life.

What do you currently do to support people you know, including people with learning disabilities, to take preventative measures to look after their health?

Here are some examples of preventative steps for people with learning disabilities as they get older.

Table 3.2: Preventive measures	
Preventing the onset of illness or injury	Early diagnosis and prompt treatment to prevent more serious illness
■ Encouraging a healthy lifestyle in adult life. ■ Encouraging a healthy lifestyle in older age. ■ Reducing the risk of falls. ■ Having an Annual Health Check to receive advice about looking after health.	■ Regular screening. ■ Having an Annual Health Check to check blood pressure, weight etc. ■ Taking medication correctly. ■ Regular medication reviews.

A key message on prevention is that if people are well supported during their adult life to make healthy choices about their diet and to have an active lifestyle, they are likely to approach older age more able to cope with the physical and mental changes that occur. Continuing to support people to eat well and be active in old age should contribute to people ageing well, both physically and mentally.

A preventative approach will not remove the risk of all illnesses, but will keep many at bay or minimise their impact. The important message to remember is that health problems can build up over many years. Think about how the preventative measures described in Table 3.2 could have a positive impact on the health problems described in Table 3.1 on page 30.

Sometimes it can feel difficult to encourage people to make healthy choices about diet and exercise and you may worry about where encouragement crosses the line into putting pressure on someone. The challenge for supporters is to find a way to encourage people in a non-judgemental way and explain the implications of making a choice. Think about how you can help someone to make an informed choice. Then you will not be taking away a person's right to make choices but supporting their right to have the information they need to make an informed choice.

Task: explaining consequences of healthy and unhealthy choices

Think about how you could explain to someone you support about the longer-term impact of making a healthy or unhealthy choice about their diet or physical activity level in a non-judgemental way. An example of this could be explaining the consequences of a sugary diet, for example using story boards to show how sugar leads to putting on weight, which in turn can lead to finding activities more difficult such as climbing the stairs at home. This may lead to needing to move home because of no longer being able to get upstairs to their bedroom. Alternatively, you could look at how to explain the positive changes that should follow from replacing unhealthy snacks with healthy ones.

Write down your ideas or prepare a resource to share with the person.

3. Good support to get the right healthcare in later life

There are a number of ways in which support staff can contribute to people getting the right healthcare as they get older. These are some of the actions that can be taken to help people get the right healthcare.

- Being observant to changes in people's body language or behaviour, and recording and responding to these.

- Sharing accessible information for people to understand about their health.

- Providing consistent support at appointments.

- Making sure people have a person-centred and up-to-date Health Action Plan.

- Creating person-centred information to take to health appointments and when going to stay in hospital (known as a Hospital Passport).

- Bringing in the skills of learning disability health experts (e.g. speech and language therapists, community nurses, physiotherapists, learning disability liaison nurses).

- Timely medication reviews.

- Advocating for reasonable adjustments.

Do you think these are already part of your practice? If not, should you or your service be thinking about them? Also, there may be other approaches not mentioned above that you are already using. If so, make a note of these.

There are many obstacles to people receiving good support in hospital, one of the biggest being the failure of health services to make 'reasonable adjustments'.

Reflection

What do you understand by the term 'reasonable adjustments'?

Here is information from the GOV.UK website:

Under the Equality Act 2010 public sector organisations have to make changes in their approach or provision to ensure that services are accessible to disabled people as well as everybody else. Reasonable adjustments can mean alterations to buildings but may also mean changes to policies, procedures and staff training to ensure that services work equally well for people with learning disabilities.

This may mean:

■ clear, simple and possibly repeated explanations of what's happening and of treatments

■ help with appointments

Public sector organisations shouldn't simply wait and respond to difficulties as they emerge: the duty on them is 'anticipatory', meaning they have to think about what's likely to be needed in advance.

All organisations that provide NHS or adult social care must follow the accessible information standard by law. The standard aims to make sure that people who have a disability, impairment or sensory loss are provided with information that they can easily read or understand with support so they can communicate effectively with health and social care services.

www.gov.uk/government/publications/reasonable-adjustments-a-legal-duty/

The task below uses the story of Kamal, who has a planned operation for an eye cataract, and aims to help you think about good practice in supporting people to receive the right healthcare. In the exercise that follows, remember to include any 'reasonable adjustments' you think might help Kamal.

 ## Task: Kamal's story

Read Kamal's story and then answer the questions below.

Kamal's story

Kamal is 62 years old and lives in a house with two friends. There is always support at the house in the daytime and a support worker sleeps in at night. Kamal has anxiety and depression and takes anti-depressants. Over the last few years staff have noticed that Kamal was doing less around the flat, was generally not very confident when walking around, and was becoming withdrawn. He went for an eye test and was diagnosed with a cataract which gradually got worse and now requires surgery. Kamal is very anxious about going to hospital and having the operation but he understands he needs to do something as his sight is getting worse and he has said he will have the operation. Kamal needs time to process information and he finds pictorial information helpful as he can return to it a number of times.

On a piece of paper, write down your ideas about what staff could do to help Kamal:

- before he has his operation
- at the hospital on the day of his operation
- after care when he is back home.

You may find that your longest list will be in the section 'before he has his operation'.

Once you have written your ideas, look at *Table 3.3: Ideas to support Kamal* and compare it with your list. An important point to note is that carrying out an internet search often leads to useful Easy Read information which can be shared with the person or used to give information in a way that works for them. The charity SeeAbility had detailed information about eye care on their website which contributed ideas for Kamal's care.

Table 3.3: Ideas to support Kamal

Before the operation	■ Hospital passport with a one-page summary of information relevant to health staff for cataract operation.
	■ One-page profile of Kamal – ask if he would like it to be shared with hospital staff, both medical and reception staff.
	■ Find out what he wants to know about the day of the operation e.g. would he like to visit the hospital beforehand, does he want to know the details of the operation?
	■ Create a story board of what will happen on the day.
	■ Think about whether Kamal has any cultural or religious needs in relation to his hospital visit.
	■ Use literature from relevant organisations, such as the RNIB, to understand what will happen on the day and during aftercare, and use this to give Kamal the information he wants or for staff to know and be prepared.
	■ Look for Easy Read information (when you search 'people with learning disabilities and cataract operations' you find SeeAbility has produced Easy Read information about cataract operations. They have also created an Eye Surgery Support Plan).
	■ Plan support hours so that support staff who know him well and help him cope with his anxiety are supporting him the day before, on the day of the operation itself, and the next day. Let him know who will be with him.
	■ Find out his past experiences of hospital appointments and treatments and find out what worked/didn't work.

continued ➜

Before the operation (cont'd)	■ Ask him and others who know him well what might help him to relax e.g something to listen to or hold.
	■ Think about what reasonable adjustments, under the Equality Act, may be needed. An example of this could be asking the consultant or booking clerk if Kamal can have the first operation of the day (if that would help with his anxiety).
	■ Find out if the hospital has a Learning Disability Liaison Nurse.
	■ Ask Kamal if he has any questions he would like to ask the consultant when he has a pre-op assessment. Write them down in Easy Read so he can take them with him.
	■ Discuss at the pre-op appointment whether additional sedation is an option and explain this to Kamal.
At the hospital	■ Make sure he has his hospital passport and one-page profile with him.
	■ You could ask to be alerted when Kamal leaves the operating theatre so support staff can be with him in the recovery suite.
Aftercare	■ Plan the aftercare beforehand with Kamal – ask if he would like this written down in a way he understands and can think about.
	■ Explain that after surgery he will need to be still for the length of time the consultant has said. Find out what he would like to do in that time – is there an activity he would enjoy that would be distracting?
	■ Before the operation, explain to Kamal about eyedrops and an eye patch, which will be part of his aftercare – ask Kamal if he would like to practice wearing the eyepatch beforehand and try out eyedrops using Artificial Tears.
	■ Plan additional support if Kamal needs one-to-one support afterwards to be still.
	■ Be observant during Kamal's period of recovery and if there are any causes for concern or changes in Kamal's well-being, seek medical advice as he may not be able to indicate pain, be aware of infection or any other problems.

Reflection

Think about how you might adapt and use the template for Kamal's operation within your service or organisation?

Your learning from this chapter

To finish, complete the summary below.

These are the main points that I have learnt from this chapter and would like to use to develop my practice:

Resources and references

Look on the internet for Easy Read information on specific health problems often produced by specialist health organisations or charities. In addition, the website EasyHealth (www.easyhealth.org.uk/) has Easy Read health leaflets, videos and advice.

There are many Books Beyond Words publications about health including Going into Hospital, Getting on with Type 2 Diabetes, Looking after my Heart, Looking after my Eyes. For more information, see: https://booksbeyondwords. co.uk/bookshop/

Preventing falls in people with learning disabilities: making reasonable adjustments
www.gov.uk/government/publications/preventing-falls-in-people-with-learning-disabilities

Learning Disabilities Mortality Review Programme (LeDeR) has produced helpful resources for social care providers including sepsis, constipation, aspiration pneumonia and recognising deterioration. They also produce an annual report. http://www.bristol.ac.uk/sps/leder/resources/information-and-resources-for-social-care-providers-/

Chapter 4: Being active and involved

Aim and learning outcomes

The aim of this chapter is to provide ideas and approaches for supporting people to be active and involved in later life.

It will help you to:

- understand the importance of supporting people to remain as active and involved with other people and in their community as they wish to
- gain tools to support people to be as active and involved as they wish to be, both at home and in the community
- know how to support decision-making in older age.

Introduction: being active and involved in later life

Support workers have an important role in supporting people to remain as active and involved with other people in their community as they wish to be. It is very easy for people to become more isolated as they get older and this has many repercussions for people's emotional well-being and their physical health. Being active and connected with others also increases a person's support network, which has many benefits and may reduce their dependence on paid supporters.

Look at Figure 4.1 on page 40 and follow what happens to Sunita once she begins to find it difficult to go out in the evening. She begins to lose contact with her friends and particularly her close friend Hanifa. Over time she loses confidence and decides to stop another activity leading to loneliness and a low level of depression.

Compare this with Figure 4.2 that follows, where Sunita makes the same decision but her support worker finds out her reason for deciding not to go to the club as well as what is important to Sunita (chiefly, seeing her close friend). She uses this to organise Sunita's support to keep her connected with Hanifa and the club and also introduces a new person, a volunteer driver, into Sunita's support network. Sunita remains confident and continues with her other activities.

Figure 4.1:

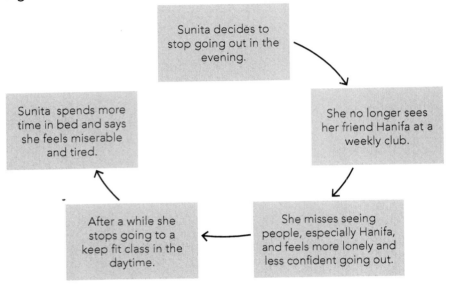

Figure 4.2:

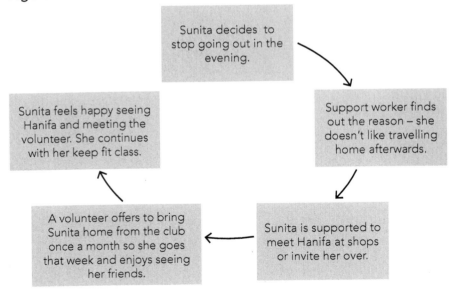

This is a simple example of how a support worker's actions can have a positive impact on a person's life which will have ongoing implications for her as she gets increasingly older. Some people may want to become less active as they get older but it's beneficial not to assume this is the case and to explore with the person what is happening for them.

In this chapter there are three exercises that explore aspects of supporting people to be active and involved, with information for you to read and a number of short tasks to complete:

1. Being connected to others.

2. Adapting activities to maintain involvement.

3. Making decisions.

1. Being connected to others

This exercise builds on the ideas discussed in the chapter's introduction, about the importance of being connected with other people. Loneliness and social isolation often increase as people get older for a variety of reasons. Loneliness is one of the main causes of low mood and depression, which can have a major effect on a person's motivation and independence.

The Care Act (2014) recognises the importance of relationships in people's lives as it has, as one of its outcomes that is eligible for funding, the right to maintain and develop family or other personal relationships if the lack of these would have 'a significant impact on the person's well-being'.

Reflection

Think about why people might become less connected as they grow older. Think about your family and friends as well as people you support.

Here are some of the possible reasons:

- Retiring from work or stopping voluntary work.

- Difficulty travelling to social clubs or activities.

- Increasing anxiety about going out.

- Becoming too frail to go out.

- Parents and friends may be less able to travel to meet up or visit.

- Contact with friends may be lost, for example if they move out of a shared house.

Now watch **Film Clip 4.1: Friendship** in which Ian talks about the importance of friendship.

Then watch **Film Clip 4.2: Lack of friendship** in which Christine talks about an older man who only had paid staff in his life.

Finally, watch **Film Clip 4.3: As needs change**.

Gloria, who is mentioned in the film, has a progressive illness, uses a reclining wheelchair and lives in a lot of pain, but a few simple ideas have helped her to stay connected with people who are important to her.

Read through the table below to gain ideas about how people may lose connections as they get older, and to learn some actions that can be taken to help people stay connected.

Table 4.1: How to keep people connected with others

	Reasons people may lose connections as they get older	Suggestions to maintain existing connections or build new connections
Family	■ Parents may have died or be very elderly themselves, they may have mobility difficulties or health problems making it difficult to travel or to have their son or daughter to stay. ■ Other family members, such as siblings, cousins, nieces and nephews, may not be sure how to be involved in a person's life and be supportive.	■ Look for alternative ways to be in touch with elderly relatives such as using on-line video (e.g. Skype), phone calls, support to send cards and presents. ■ If parents have died, find out how the person would like to keep their memories alive, for example having a memory box and acknowledging anniversaries. ■ Give support to build contacts with other family members such as siblings, cousins, nieces and nephews. Give support to collect and share contact details. ■ Find out from the person you support how they would like family members to be involved in their life and share ideas with family members. Some ideas to look at include: whether they would like to be included in family events, share an interest together, reminisce together about family life, become an advocate at reviews or when decisions need to be made.

continued ➜

	Reasons people may lose connections as they get older	Suggestions to maintain existing connections or build new connections
Friends	■ Friends may be ageing themselves and finding it difficult to go out or meet up. ■ Younger friends may be getting impatient with the person becoming slower and less keen to spend time together. ■ Friends may have moved away or died. ■ Shared interests with friends may have changed as they have both got older.	■ Talk to the person about their friends or find out by using a relationship map (see link in resources at end of the chapter) with people who know them well. ■ Support the person to create a phone book with friends' names and contact details and make sure this is kept up to date. Use the book to talk with the person about their friends and what they might like to do together – give support to arrange this. Find out who shares an interest. ■ Give support to invite friends over and to visit friends – help to get this pattern established before either finds travelling difficult. If transport, such as a taxi is needed, ask for this to be put into a care and support plan. ■ Support someone to organise an activity at their house e.g. a friend or group of friends come to do a craft activity, watch football, have a pizza.
Work/volunteering	■ Reached retirement age. ■ Retired because job has become too difficult. ■ Stopped volunteering because it became too tiring. ■ Finding the journey difficult.	■ Use work skills to find a volunteering role, become involved in a community project or do something for a friend or neighbour. ■ Look for more manageable job or voluntary work/negotiate fewer hours. ■ Arrange to keep in touch with ex-work mates, sharing contact details and keeping in touch with anyone who was a friend at work. ■ Look for a valued role somewhere else, such as becoming a trustee of a local charity, joining an advocacy group, becoming a quality checker in a health or social care service. continued ➜

	Reasons people may lose connections as they get older	Suggestions to maintain existing connections or build new connections
People and places in the community	■ Difficulties traveling to places. ■ Activities become tiring. ■ Changing interests with age. ■ Need to leave a centre or service because of age criteria. ■ Centres or services not making reasonable adjustments or being inclusive of people as they get older. ■ Other people in community places lack the patience to slow down and give the person the time they need.	■ Look for activities in the community for older people, either specific for people with learning disabilities or open to everyone e.g. healthy walks, lunch clubs, singing groups, classes. ■ Depending on the person's ability, or with the help of their support worker, the person can help a community activity to become more inclusive of people with a learning disability. ■ Give support to the person to say hello, chat or become involved with other people at the activity so that they don't just go along but fail to connect with others there.

Task: keeping people connected

Now access online *Learning Resource 2: Your ideas to support someone you know to keep connected with others* and use the template to think about someone you support who may have lost, or be at risk of losing, connections. Use the first column to note the changes. Then use the second column to write down any ideas you could try in order to overcome some of these changes, using either your own ideas or adapting ones from Table 4.1.

Once you have completed this, think about which of the ideas you would like to go back and use in your work, or discuss them with your manager, within the next few weeks. Are there ways in which you could rethink the use of your support time to build connections? An example of this could be going to a lunch-club in the local community and supporting someone to get to know other members, rather than going to eat lunch together in a pub.

2. Adapting activities as people age

As people age, their interests may change and their energy levels and ability to participate in certain activities may also diminish. It's important to have some tools to think about and understand how a person can be supported to continue to be involved even when their abilities change with age.

Some people may remain active while others will want to slow down and take things easier. You need to be aware of a person's energy levels and how these might vary at different times of the day or during the week. The important thing is to find out what works and what doesn't work for *each* person you support.

Task: Adapting an activity

The next exercise will give you a structure for thinking through what is happening for a specific person. Read Joyce's story and then answer the questions that follow.

Joyce's story

On a Friday, Joyce goes to a community centre in her local town for a line dancing class followed by a meal at the lunch club. She lives in a village and has a 40-minute bus ride to get there travelling with a support worker. Jenny has got slower walking from the bus stop to the community centre and so it is a bit of a rush to get to the class in time for the start. When she arrives, she is often stressed and rushes to the toilet. Sometimes she says she wants to stop coming. But she is much more cheerful when she hears the music and starts to join in the dance movements. She sometimes says her legs are getting tired.

Until a year ago Joyce helped to lay the tables for lunch in the half hour between her class finishing and lunch being served, but now she's no longer encouraged to do this by the lunch club as she isn't able to get it done in the time available. She usually sits on her own waiting for lunch.

At lunchtime she seems to enjoy chatting to the people sitting next to her. But on the way home she seems to be tired and anxious and when the support worker asked her what's wrong she said she thinks she might stop going to the centre as 'it's all too much'. The support worker wasn't sure what to do as she knows Joyce is at home the day before and day after, and that much of the time she seems to enjoy being at the centre.

How do you think the support worker should talk to Joyce about this and what suggestions might they explore together?

Make some notes about:

- what might be happening for Joyce and what might you want to explore with her and/or people who know her

- any options to make changes in her day that you might explore with her.

Once you have completed this, look at Table 4.2 and see how your answers compare. The ones below are only suggestions and you may have had different ideas. The important point is that you have used a process to adapt an activity to support someone to remain active and involved.

Table 4.2: Joyce's story: some ideas

Question	Suggestions
What might be happening for Joyce? What might you want to explore with her and/or the people who know her?	■ Has the bus journey become too tiring? ■ Is it the rushing rather than the journey itself that is the problem? ■ Does she get hungry or worry about incontinence when travelling? ■ Is she worried about falling over when travelling or at the class? ■ Does she miss her role of setting the tables? ■ Does she find it hard to talk to other lunch club members? Would she like to get to know some of them?
What options might you explore with her and/or people who know her?	■ Would she like to get an earlier bus so it is less of a rush and she has time for a rest, a cup of tea and to go to the toilet before the class starts? ■ Would she like to take a snack to eat on the bus? Would she like a reminder to go to the toilet before leaving home or when she arrives at the community centre? ■ Would she like to think about getting a taxi for some or all of the journey – either on those weeks when she feels tired, or all the time? Is there someone else at the class who lives nearby and could share a taxi? ■ Would she like to join the class a bit later, perhaps when there is a break so it is not so much of a rush or not so tiring? ■ Would she like to have some rests during the class? ■ Would she like to sit on a chair for part or all of the class and exercise her upper body? ■ Could she have a role, such as calling out the moves with the class teacher, when she is tired so she still feels involved? ■ Could she have a new role at the lunch club that involves sitting down? ■ Would she like support to get to know some of the other club members so she could sit with them while waiting for lunch?

Reflection

How might your service or organisation use this approach to ensure people continue to have meaningful activities and feel engaged with others as they get older?

One more thought

There may be activities in the community for older people generally or for older people who are frail or living with dementia. These services may have had little or no experience of including a person with learning disabilities. You could look at how you could approach such a service to help them welcome and include someone with learning disabilities.

3. Making decisions

Another way of enabling people to be active and involved is through supporting them to make decisions and choices about their life. Even if someone finds physical activity difficult, they can still be active and involved through making as many decisions as they feel able to about day-to-day matters and bigger questions in their life. Often the loss of physical ability is wrongly equated with a loss of cognitive ability and leads to supporters stepping in to make decisions on someone's behalf. This exercise will give you ideas about how to keep people actively involved in making decisions about their lives.

As people get older they are often faced with big decisions. These might be:

- when to retire from paid or voluntary work
- when to stop taking part in a specific activity that's enjoyable but has become difficult
- when to start using a walking aid
- whether to have or refuse a health treatment
- whether to move home
- their preferences for end-of-life care and funeral arrangements.

Reflection

What sort of emotions do you think people might feel when faced with these sorts of decisions?

Here are some suggestions:

- Worry about making a bad decision.
- Sadness to be leaving something/somewhere they like.
- Relief to be moving on from something.
- Concerned they might upset someone by making a certain decision, or worried what they might say.
- Stress that something might go wrong e.g. when having an operation.
- Confusion about possible consequences.
- Realisation that life is changing and they are becoming more dependent.

People may have a mixture of these emotions and so feel very confused. On top of this, as we get older there are often more decisions that need to be made because circumstances are more likely to be changing. It can also be the case that change happens more rapidly so there is pressure to make decisions quickly and the person is not meaningfully involved in decisions about their life. It is therefore helpful to have had conversations in advance and to have already supported people to think through options wherever possible.

Task: Good practice in decision-making

Watch **Film Clip 4.4: Giving me information** in which Ian talks about how he needs information to help him understand and make decisions. As people get older they often feel more worried or anxious about making a decision but this doesn't mean they want people to step in and make decisions for them. Time needs to be spent looking for ways of helping people to make choices so they maintain this ability for as long as possible. An important point to note is that as people get older they are likely to need much more time to think things over and will not want to be rushed.

Listening to Ian in the film clip and using your own experience, how could you give good support for both day-to-day decisions and bigger decisions? Would any of the ideas in the table below be useful?

Ideas
Give the person plenty of time.
Return to a discussion after someone has had time to think about it and/or talk to others.
Ask open and non-judgemental questions.
Provide information in different formats.
Use visual cues, story boards and photo stories.
Only give one piece of information at a time, and wait until someone is ready before giving another piece.
Involve other people who know the person well and are outside of the support organisation.

One more thought

Have you thought about the idea of people being supported to be active citizens as they grow older? What might active citizenship mean for older people with learning disabilities that you support?

Do you support people to vote in local or national elections? There is a recent example of an organisation supporting a woman, aged 81, to vote for the first time in 2015 who has since gone on to take an active interest in watching the news, has visited Parliament and voted in subsequent elections (www.dimensions-uk.org/case-study/barbaras-political-engagement/).

People could also have a role of advocating for other older people with learning disabilities or quality checking services to make sure they give good support to older people with learning disabilities.

Your learning from this chapter

To finish, complete the summary below.

> These are the main points that I have learnt from this chapter and would like to use to develop my practice:

Resources

The Thinking Ahead guide has a template for a relationship map called *People in my life*, which is free to download at: www.togethermatters.org.uk/templates-pdf/ (accessed September 2019).

Chapter 5: Home life

Aim and learning outcomes

The aim of this chapter is to understand how to adapt a person's home environment and their support to make sure it is a place where they can relax and feel safe, while maintaining as much choice and independence as possible.

It will help you to:

- know how to improve a person's home environment to make it safer and more comfortable
- gain ideas to promote a person's independence, choice and well-being at home
- gain confidence about having conversations about moving home.

Introduction: home life

As people get older, the time they spend at home should be enjoyable and fulfilling rather than a gradual slide into sitting around more and more without much sense of purpose. As covered in the previous chapter, although people's energy levels usually reduce as they get older, there are still many opportunities for people to be active and involved at home as well as in their community. This may require some creative thinking and planning about the use of support hours.

A person's home life is likely to become more important to them as they get older. Some of the reasons for this are:

- they may find it harder to go out and about
- they may have stopped work or cut down days at daytime activities
- they may choose to relax more and do quieter activities at home
- they may need to meet up with family and friends at their home so want a nice place to invite people to.

There are three exercises on the topic of home life for you to read about and do a short task:

1. Comfort and safety at home.
2. Activities at home.
3. Where will I live?

1. Comfort and safety at home

Home environments can become more uncomfortable and less safe as people get older. Some of the problems that may arise are:

- more difficult to move around or less comfortable as their body changes

- feeling less steady when moving around and possibility of falling

- less able to use hands to grip

- not seeing or hearing so well

- difficulty remembering where to find things around the house.

These changes can lead to someone feeling more anxious and uncertain in their home, which in turn can lead to increased confusion, frustration and a lowering of confidence. On the other hand, there are steps that can be taken to help someone feel safer and more comfortable, make life at home more manageable and lead to people being more confident in their home.

Watch **Film Clip 5.1: Bringing warmth**, which describes how to make someone feel more comfortable in a residential home. The changes being suggested are all quite small, easy to achieve and inexpensive, but together they made a significant difference to Marcus's life. Simple changes such as these can help to make time at home more enjoyable, fulfilling and comfortable.

Table 5.1 gives ideas for making changes at home. Read through the ideas and think about which might be useful for the environment in which you work.

Table 5.1: Making changes at home: ideas	
What difficulties is someone facing	**Ideas to consider**
Feeling cold around the house	■ Warmer bedding. ■ Having extra rugs beside the bed or on chairs. ■ Thicker curtains. ■ Heating on a slightly higher setting. ■ Cosy clothing such as thermal t-shirts and socks, fleece and sleepwear. ■ Warm coloured soft furnishings and pictures on walls. continued ➔

What difficulties is someone facing	Ideas to consider
Aches and pains when sitting in a chair or lying in bed	■ Having a good quality chair and mattress with the right level of support. ■ Having cushions and pillows for support. ■ Having foot/leg support. ■ Having a riser-recliner chair to help get in and out. ■ Having chairs with arms to give support while sitting and to use to stand up. ■ Where necessary, getting advice from specialists, such as occupational therapists, about seating and beds.
Eyesight getting poorer making it more difficult to see objects, read numbers on cooker and instructions such as recipes etc.	■ Regular eye tests. ■ Extra lighting, lamps close by where needed. ■ Maximising natural light by keeping windows clean, pulling back curtains and not placing furniture in front of windows. ■ Use of contrasting colours, uncluttered surfaces. ■ Larger print information. ■ Large faced clock. ■ Photos of people on phone rather than names. ■ Stickers.
Hearing getting worse making it more difficult to hear conversation, the doorbell, phone, TV or radio	■ Regular hearing tests. ■ Reducing background noise. ■ Having headphones to listen to music. ■ Wireless flashing doorbell.
Finding it more difficult to go to meet friends and family	■ Receiving support to invite people to their house and making it a positive experience. ■ Creating a pleasant space for visitors to sit, have a cup of tea or a meal, do activities together. ■ Using on-line video calls, such as Skype.
Helping to reduce trips and falls	■ Storage space to remove clutter from the floor. ■ Keeping top and bottom of stairs clear. ■ Enough sockets so electric leads do not run over the floor. ■ Grab rails to hold onto when moving around such as by the toilet, on stairs and steps, fitting a second bannister. ■ Easy Read fall prevention advice. ■ Call alert – can be to another room in the property or to a call centre. ■ Occupational Therapy assessment. continued →

What difficulties is someone facing	Ideas to consider
Finding it harder to grip things, open containers, pick things up from the floor, take food out of the oven or microwave, stand while cooking etc.	■ Adaptations such as lever taps, easy-grip kitchen utensils. ■ Easy-reach grabbers to pick things up. ■ Kettle tipper. ■ Perching stool to have support in a near-standing position.
Finding it hard to remember things such as where to find things, when to take medication or to have regular drinks.	■ Assistive technology such as a call alert, reminders to take medication. ■ Hooks in obvious places to hang keys, coats or bags but not visible through the front door or letterbox. ■ Ask people about how they would like to store things such as clothes and food, so this fits with any changes to way they do things. ■ Store things in clear containers. ■ Encourage people to keep things in same place and reduce clutter. ■ Have a whiteboard or magnetic board.
Finding it hard to relax	■ Supporting people to access relaxing music or relaxation tapes. ■ Look at *Talking Together: Facilitating peer support activities to help people with learning disabilities understand about growing older and living with dementia*, which has two activities to help people relax: Activity 16: Relaxation, and Activity 17: Music and relaxation (www.togethermatters.org.uk)
Carrying shopping	■ Look at online shopping and home delivery.
All areas	■ Considering whether an Occupational Therapy, Speech and Language Therapy or Physiotherapy assessment could be helpful and make a referral. ■ Use resources and information for people who are getting older, living with a disability and/or dementia, such as the Disabled Living Foundation (dlf.org.uk), Age UK and the Alzheimer's Society (see Resources at end of chapter).

Watch **Film Clip 5.2: Staying safe** to hear the changes Ian has made to keep safe in his home because of his sight difficulties.

 ## Task: Changes at home

Have a look at *Learning Resource 3: Making changes at home: template*. Think about someone you support and use the left-hand column to identify any relevant issues for the person (you could highlight these) and use the right-hand column to note ideas you think might help them to have a better home environment. You could tap into your own experience of making your own home environment, or that of older family members, feel comfortable and homely.

What will you go away and do? Write down those ideas that you intend to follow up with a person or people you support, along with the first step to start this.

One more thought

How might you gather information about the changes people might find helpful in their home? If it is a shared house or a residential home, could a few people walk around together with a prompt list to look at different features or rooms and suggest changes they would like e.g. hooks on the wall to hang up bags so people know where to find them and don't fall over them on the floor. An activity 'Creating a friendly environment' is available in *Talking Together: Facilitating peer support activities to help people with learning disabilities understand about growing older and living with dementia* (available at www. togethermatters.org.uk).

2. Activities at home

Support workers play an invaluable role in helping people to be involved with daily living and leisure activities at home, which encourages their independence, makes life enjoyable and promotes their well-being.

Think about whether you have noticed that people you support have found activities around the house more difficult as they have lost physical or cognitive skills as part of the ageing process. What examples have you noticed or do you think might occur?

Some examples might be:

- Carrying things up and down stairs.

- Not being able to read labels and so being unsure whether they are using the right ingredients or cleaning products.

- Finding the vacuum cleaner too heavy to move around.

- Taking out the recycling (walking and carrying).

- Standing up for long enough to cook a meal.

Every person will be different in relation to what they find harder and the extent to which this happens. Sometimes people will cover up what they are finder harder, but you may learn about them when you talk to people about their experience of growing older, as discussed in Chapter 2.

Task: Understanding people's changing needs

One approach to understanding about people's changing needs is to find out, in a fairly structured way, what they are still managing to do and what is becoming more difficult, and then planning support in relation to this information. Someone may not feel able to do any part of a task on their own, but if someone is alongside to guide them, or by using approaches such as hand over hand, they may still be able to participate in the task.

You could break down different parts of a task and find out whether a person feels they:

- can continue doing it on their own

- can do parts of a task, but need support with other parts

- need support while doing all of the task but would like to continue doing it

- no longer feel able to do it and would like someone else to do it.

The aim of this approach is not to force people to keep doing things, but to offer support to encourage as much independence and control over their home life as they would like as well as keeping them physically active and maintaining their confidence.

Another way to be active and engaged at home is through activities that support a person's well-being. The nature of these activities will vary depending on a person's interests and how they engage with a task. Below are two examples of how an activity can contribute to a person's well-being.

Planting indoor bulbs	Listening to pieces of music
Learning a new skill/having a new interest	Making choices
Connecting to living things	Learning about new pieces of music
Responsibility/nurturing	Sensory stimulation
Enjoyment	Relaxation
Relaxation	Sharing pleasure of music with others
Growing things to share with others	

Task: Active and engaged at home

Having read about different ideas to support people to be active and engaged at home, how do you think these might be used where you work and what ideas will you take back and share with others?

At your place of work, would it be helpful to use an Easy Read list of tasks, or photos of different tasks, to ask people what bits they still feel confident to do, which they feel able to do with more help and which they no longer feel able to do? Could people who live in a shared flat or house look at this together and think about how they could add another option of supporting each other to do tasks?

If you are supporting someone with profound and multiple learning disabilities, are there steps you could take to increase their opportunities for sensory and relaxation activities?

3. Where will I live?

In Chapter 4 we looked at the big decisions that sometimes face people in older age. It is often a time when people have to think about the suitability of where they live or are faced with a fairly immediate need to move. Moving home can be a sensitive subject and sometimes one that is avoided unless absolutely necessary. But this means people may be faced with moving in a crisis without ever having talked to anyone about what would be important to them if they had to move. Or they may be living with worry about having to move to somewhere new as they get older but don't know how to talk about this.

One of the discussions that often takes place is whether someone should be supported to grow older where they live, with changes being made to their environment and their support, or whether moving to a new environment and/or with support more geared to their changing needs is preferable. There is no easy answer to this and will depend on the person and what will make life better for them. It's important that the needs of the person and those they may live with are paramount. Exploring with a person their options for housing and support in advance of needing to move should help people, and others who know them well, to make more informed choices.

Task: Difficult choices

Watch **Film Clip 5.3: Where will I live?**, in which Ian talks about where he might live in the future, and then read through the worries that he has.

- 'In the future there will be big decisions to take, such as where I might live.'

- 'Will someone do an assessment and say I should no longer be living on my own but need to live in a home?'

- 'When I can't live on my own anymore, life changes completely. What would a home be like? Will I have enough money – how will it work?'

- 'I want to be somewhere I can stay safe but I also want to live on my own as long as possible.'

Think about what you could do to support Ian with his worries right now, as well as what you could do as time passes and he may need to move home. Write down three or four ideas for what you might do and why.

Ian has a lot of independence, but if you support people who would find the concept of a move more difficult, how might you use your learning from this exercise to support them?

If you are supporting people living at home with family carers you may want to support the person and their family to develop an emergency plan (e.g. in case a family carer becomes ill). Watch **Film Clip 5.4: Emergency plans** to understand their importance. Further details about emergency plans are in *Thinking Ahead: a planning guide for families* (see Resources on p62).

Your learning from this chapter

To finish, complete the summary below.

These are the main points that I have learnt from this chapter and would
like to use to develop my practice:

Resources

Making Your Home Dementia Friendly from the Alzheimer's Society: www.
alzheimers.org.uk/sites/default/files/migrate/downloads/making_your_home_
dementia_friendly.pdf (accessed September 2019).

Talking Together, Activities 16 and 17: www.togethermatters.org.uk/talking-
together-pdf/ (accessed September 2019).

Adapting Your Home from Age UK: www.ageuk.org.uk/globalassets/age-uk/
documents/information-guides/ageukig17_adapting_your_home_inf.pdf
(accessed September 2019).

Thinking Ahead: A planning guide for families, Section 7: Making an
Emergency Plan. There is also a blank form to make a plan in the templates
section. For more information, see: www.togethermatters.org.uk/resources-and-
information/

Chapter 6: Bereavement and dying

Aim and learning outcomes

The aim of this chapter is to provide an understanding of how to give good support on issues relating to bereavement and dying.

It will help you to:

- understand the importance of talking about difficult subjects such as bereavement and dying

- learn practical skills and tools to communicate about bereavement and dying

- understand your own training and support needs when supporting people with learning disabilities around bereavement and dying.

Introduction: bereavement and dying

This chapter will give you an understanding of how to give good support on issues relating to bereavement and dying.

One of the most difficult subjects to talk about or explore with someone is loss and dying, either in relation to themselves or people they know. People, generally, are often afraid to talk about death, and there is an even greater fear of having these conversations with people who have learning disabilities.

Why might you (or others) avoid having these conversations? Write down two or three points.

Did you suggest the following ideas?

- To protect people from something they may worry about and dwell on.

- You don't feel you have the right skills to talk about bereavement and dying.

- You worry that once a conversation is opened up a lot more questions will follow which may be hard to deal with.

- You feel unfamiliar with the cultural and religious/spiritual beliefs that someone might have.

However, when supporting people with learning disabilities who are ageing, bereavement and dying are topics that are going to come up in their lives and support workers will need to have the tools and confidence to involve people in 'conversations' in a way that works for them.

There are three topics around bereavement and dying for you to read about and to complete short tasks:

■ Difficult conversations: loss, bereavement and dying.

■ The significance of funerals.

■ Looking after yourself.

1. Difficult conversations: loss, bereavement and dying

Watch **Film clip 6.1: Talk to me**. How do you think a person might pick up that a parent or friend has a terminal illness even if they are not told?

Here are some suggestions:

■ The person who is ill may be physically changing, may be angry or down, have less energy and are spending more time asleep, behaving differently such as not going out to usual places, and going out less.

■ The family and friends of a person who is ill may start using different tones of voice and facial expressions, phoning or visiting more, having hushed conversations, using different body language, looking sad or upset.

■ Support staff of someone who is ill may start having more meetings or discussions, rearranging support to cover hospital appointments or visits, using a different tone of voice, facial expressions and body language with the person, and looking sad or upset.

What reasons would you give for involving people in what is happening when someone important to them is seriously ill, nearing the end of their life or has died? Think back to Clip 6.1 about having an important relationship with her mother yet being excluded.

Look at the possible reasons in Table 6.1 and use the righthand column to say whether you agree with them.

Table 6.1: Including people

Reasons for including people	What do you think?
It is their right to know that something is happening that affects them, and to express their emotions and receive or give support.	
They should not be denied the opportunity to learn coping skills: skills are learnt step by step and it is easier if these can begin to be developed with a person they are not too close to. It may help to be slightly more prepared when someone close to them is ill or dies or they are faced with their own serious or terminal illness.	
Being silent gives the wrong message about expressing emotions, implying that they should be bottled up, which in turn can lead to mental ill health and changes in behaviour.	
Avoiding difficult subjects can make people unsafe if they think their feelings don't count: people need to know they can talk about difficult things and will be supported (e.g. feeling down, being abused).	
People often have a smaller network of people in their life and are often in a dependent relationship. Therefore, individual relationships are likely to have a greater significance.	
They may be losing an important role in their life such as being a son, daughter, partner or best friend. They may also have been a carer for the person so would additionally be losing that role.	
It is likely to be more frightening and distressing not to know what's going on: the person who is ill may be changing physically and emotionally, which could be scarier to see if it is not known that the person is ill.	
Other – add other reasons that you think are important.	

The biggest barrier to talking to people about death and dying is people's fear of their lack of skills and knowledge about the best way of doing this, and concern about causing people distress. The 'Breaking Bad News' approach is very helpful in building up skills and understanding. It emphasises that helping people to understand difficult subjects is a process not a one-off event, so people with learning disabilities can be supported over the period of time they need. It advocates the idea of giving people 'small, singular chunks of information', the size of which would depend on the person. Sometimes when we are talking about something difficult we tend to do the opposite and rush through information in the hope of getting it over and done with. The Breaking Bad News approach gives much more value to helping someone understand, and each chunk of information is seen as 'building a foundation of knowledge', the process of which is summarised in the box below.

Building a foundation of knowledge

- Break complex information down into singular, discrete chunks of information. A seemingly simple statement (e.g. 'Mum has cancer') usually encapsulates a vast range of background knowledge, as well as knowledge about immediate and future changes and implications.

- The size of the chunk depends on the person. Some people can cope with larger ones; others need them broken down further.

- Give the person these chunks of information one by one, in order to build a solid foundation of knowledge. Additional information can be given as the person's foundation of knowledge grows.

- Consider what 'background knowledge' the person already has. This will depend on the person's life experience and world view as well as their intellectual capacity.

- New information needs to make sense to the person. To someone whose primary way of understanding is through experience or objects of reference, verbal explanations will not make sense. People with severe cognitive limitations may never be able to understand the future. Decide whether it is important that the person understands this information now. This could be the case if he needs to be involved in treatment decisions, or if the information is related to immediate changes (such as a sudden death in the family).

(Taken from www.breakingbadnews.org/the-guidelines/)

What are your thoughts on this approach? Will you use the link to look at further information on the Breaking Bad News website?

2. Involvement in funerals

Funerals vary widely between different cultures and religions, but are usually ceremonies connected with the final disposition of a dead body, such as a burial or cremation, and therefore lead to many feelings of physical and emotional discomfort connected with death. Yet, for many people, they are an important ceremony.

What do you think are the secular (non-religious) reasons for attending a funeral ceremony?

Write down why you have attended a funeral or perhaps encouraged people you support to do so.

Did your suggestions include some of the following?

- An opportunity for mourning (expressing sorrow).
- An opportunity to say goodbye.
- To celebrate a person's life.
- To show sympathy and support to people close to the person who has died.
- To share your feelings of sadness and loss with others who knew the person.

Now read Lloyd's story in the box below.

Lloyd's story

Lloyd is 56 and his close friend Ben has died. Ben lived at home with his family and Lloyd lives in a house he shares with two other people. Lloyd had support to visit Ben at the hospital and hospice so he saw the changes in his friend, but support workers are not sure how much Lloyd understands when he was told Ben had died. A support worker has asked Lloyd if he would like to go Ben's funeral and he has indicated he doesn't want to go. However, the worker isn't sure if Lloyd understood what a funeral is or if he has had enough information to make a choice as to why he might go or not go. She isn't sure what to do next.

Lloyd has never been to a funeral. When his older sister died his family didn't want him to go to her funeral as they thought it would upset him. Lloyd uses a few spoken words and can answer simple questions, but often likes things explained with images and objects as well as words.

Task: Going to a funeral

Sometimes people are asked if they want to go to a funeral and are faced with making a decision without knowing what a funeral is and why they might go. They may also have picked up other people's feelings that a funeral would be too upsetting for them. Use your learning about the Breaking Bad News approach to breaking down chunks of information, and being an active listener (chapter 2), to think about what you could suggest to Lloyd's support worker. You might want to think about:

- Finding out about Lloyd's understanding of 'dying' and of funerals.

- Explaining to Lloyd what happens at a funeral and why people sometimes choose to go or not to go.

- Giving Lloyd some other options to say goodbye to his friend instead of going, or as well as going, to Ben's funeral.

You could use pens and paper if you want to draw some ideas as well as write down your thoughts. Be creative in thinking about how to do this with Lloyd and take into account that he uses only a few words.

Once you have completed this, think about how you might use your learning from this exercise at your place of work.

3. Looking after yourself

All staff need good support and training on issues of loss, bereavement and dying to enable them to engage with people and to help with their own emotions and limit the impact on their well-being. Sometimes this kind of work will bring up their own feelings of loss and memories, whether in their personal life or at work.

Think about how the previous exercise about funerals made you feel.

What support have you found helpful in the past or what do you think could be helpful? Go through the list below and decide how important you think the different statements are.

Suggestions for training, development and support	Would you find this helpful (and how)?
Training to better understand grief: to give support to people with learning disabilities and to understand your own feelings.	
Training on developing 'advance care plans' and the Mental Capacity Act to develop your understanding of decision-making.	
Opportunities to discuss bereavement and death within supervision and through on the job support.	
Receiving good support when discussing funeral planning, making a will and end of life care with people you support. Being given the necessary time ('it needs the time it will take') to talk with people you support about their death or that of others.	

continued →

Suggestions for training, development and support	Would you find this helpful (and how)?
An adequate level of staff being available when supporting someone who is dying or after someone has died.	
Being able to ask for, and receiving, additional time off after supporting someone on a difficult journey (whether with their own illness or that of someone they care about or live with).	
Being given space to reflect on and review what has been learnt, for example after someone has died.	
Receiving training on the Breaking Bad News approach.	
Other ideas.	

Do you think you and/or your team or organisation have any other more general training needs as result of this chapter?

Your learning from this chapter

To finish, complete the summary below.

These are the main points that I have learnt from this chapter and would like to use to develop my practice:

Learning Resource 1: Hopes and wishes

	How you might do this?
What communication tools will you use to ask about their hopes and wishes (e.g. what words and phrases, photos, pictures, objects)?	
What would be a good setting to ask someone (e.g. on their own, with others to share ideas, in a place where they feel relaxed/can reflect)?	
Who else might you involve (family, friends, others who know them well)?	
How will you record what they tell you and make a plan to achieve it (e.g. pictures, voices, photographs)?	
What will you do first?	

Learning Resource 2: Your ideas to support someone you know to keep connected with others

	What has / might become difficult as they get older?	What could you do to maintain existing connections or build new ones?
Family		
Friends		
Work/ volunteering		
People and places in the community		

Learning Resource 3: Making changes at home: template

What difficulties is someone facing?	Ideas to consider
Feeling cold around the house	
Aches and pains when sitting in a chair or lying in bed	
Eyesight getting poorer making it more difficult, for example, to see objects, read numbers on cooker and instructions such as recipes	
Hearing getting worse making it more difficult to hear the phone, radio or TV or conversations	
Finding it more difficult to go out and wanting to invite family and friends to visit them	
More shaky walking around and at risk of trips and falls	
Harder to grip things, open containers, pick things up from the floor	
Harder to remember things such as where to find things, when to take medication or to have regular drinks	
Other	
Finding it hard to relax	
Carrying shopping	

Further resources

Together Matters has a number of free resources on their website that will be useful when planning in a person-centred way, having conversations with people about growing older and for services to evaluate and improve their support to people as they grow older:

- *Talking Together: facilitating peer support activities to help people with learning disabilities understand about growing older and living with dementia*

- *Thinking Ahead: a planning guide for families*

- *I'm Thinking Ahead*

- *Planning Ahead: supporting families to shape the future after a diagnosis of dementia*

- *Growing Older Evaluation Toolkit: an assessment tool and action plan to improve the quality of life for people with learning disabilities as they grow older*

http://www.togethermatters.org.uk/resources-and-information/

The British Institute of Learning Disabilities (BILD) have a programme of work called Ageing Well with a range of free resources including Easy-read information on dementia and ageing well. A short film is also available on active ageing in which people talk about what helps them to keep active. In partnership with NDTi they have produced *Supporting older people with learning disabilities: a toolkit for health and social care commissioners.*

http://www.bild.org.uk/resources/ageingwell/resources/

The National Institute for Health and Care Excellence (NICE) produced guidelines *Care and support of people growing older with learning disabilities* (2018). They cover health, social care and housing in relation to the work of commissioners, practitioners and support providers.

https://www.nice.org.uk/guidance/ng96

Books Beyond Words produce books to support communication with people who find pictures easier to understand than words. Many of their titles may be useful when helping people to understand unfamiliar situations and changes in their lives, such as *Going into Hospital, Am I going to die?, When Mum Died, Ann has Dementia, Looking After my Heart, Looking after my balls, Looking after my eyes.*

https://booksbeyondwords.co.uk/

Breaking Bad News has very useful guidance about how to support people with learning disabilities in bad news situations which could be used in many aspects of life when growing older. There is guidance to show how to break down pieces of news into manageable chunks and also Ten top tips for breaking bad news.

http://www.breakingbadnews.org/

There are two sets of service standards that, although written more generally for all adults, are helpful tools for support providers to use to evaluate and improve how the support people as they grow older:

- PMLD Link developed a set of standards to ensure people with profound and multiple learning disabilities have access to consistent high-quality support throughout their lives. *Supporting people with profound and multiple learning disabilities: core and essential service standards* can be downloaded at http://www.pmldlink.org.uk/

- Paradigm are an organisation that produced the REACH standards which have become a recognised set of voluntary standards for supported living. There are nine standards that cover the key aspects of living an ordinary life and are a useful tool for individuals and organisations to be aspirational about providing support https://paradigm-uk.org/